THE WISDOM OF SAINT FRANCIS

Edited and
introduced by
Brother Ramon SSF

LION
Giftlines

This edition copyright © 1997 Lion Publishing

Published by
Lion Publishing plc
Sandy Lane West, Oxford, England
ISBN 0 7459 3644 X

First edition 1997
10 9 8 7 6 5 4 3 2 1

A catalogue record for this book is available from the British Library

Printed and bound in Singapore

Series editor: Philip Law
Project editor: Angela Handley
Book designer: Nicholas Rous
Jacket designer: Gerald Rogers

Text Acknowledgments

Extracts in *The Wisdom of Saint Francis* from the various Franciscan publications
are found together in the edited *Omnibus of Sources*: Marion A. Habig (editor),
Chicago, Illinois: Franciscan Herald Press (1971) and SPCK (1979).

Picture Acknowledgments

1 (il trapasso), 11 & 28 (la visione dei troni), 17 (il dono del mantello),
25 & cover (la predica agli uccelli), 33 (il miracolo della fonte),
39 (le stimmate), 41 (l'estasi): Giotto (1266–1336), details from
'Storie di S. Francesco', la Basilica di S. Francesco, Assisi.

2/3 (la rinuncia ai beni), 4, 8 & 21 (benedizione ai consoli di Bevagna e
Montefalco), 23 (le esequie): Gozzoli Benozzo (1420–1497), details from
'Storie di S. Francesco', S. Francesco, Montefalco.

15: Orcagna Andrea (sec. XIV), Trionfo della morte – p. (mendicanti),
S. Croce (Museo), Firenze.

46: S. Chiara con otto storie, S. Chiara, Assisi.

Artwork

Jane Thomson and Amanda Barlow

CONTENTS

INTRODUCTION

St Francis of Assisi was an amazing man. He was born in 1182 and died in 1226, but in those forty-four years he turned the world upside down, as his master Jesus had done before him.

He is a universal man, not only loved in all parts of the church, but revered by all people of all creeds and none. Why is this? Because he manifested genuine joy, simplicity and compassion. His joy overflowed because he felt the upsurge of the love of God within his heart; his simplicity marked his common life because he held on to nothing that was superfluous; his compassion led him not only to nurse lepers, but to love every sentient creature – indeed, the whole of creation.

Hundreds of books and papers have been

written about him, but I want to say four things about his spirituality which reveal his attractiveness and relevance to our poor world.

First, Francis was a man of Jesus. After his youthful searching restlessness, one day the image of the crucified Jesus at the chapel of San Damiano spoke to him. Francis responded joyfully, tearfully, gladly, and from that moment, at twenty-three years of age, he became enamoured and intoxicated by the love, the joy and the wonder of the living Jesus. Christ radiated from him, and his living, preaching and healing all flowed from that inward source of peace and love. Towards the end of his life he entered into such mystical union with Christ that he received in his body the *stigmata*, the sacred wounds of Jesus, in hands, feet and side. Although he endeavoured to hide these wounds, people became aware of the passion and beauty of Jesus within him.

Second, Francis was a man of simplicity. To let go all that is not absolutely needful, and to

give everything else away seems madness in our materialistic, acquisitive society. That is why Francis is both relevant and revered in his genuine integrity. He was not an ascetic, but simply a man who identified with the poor Jesus, and because he was convinced of the spiritual riches of love and joy, he was able to share everything with everyone. He was simply human, simply basic, simply open to men, women and children, to birds and beasts and all creation.

Third, Francis was a man of contemplation. This does not only mean that he loved to pray to his heavenly Father, but that he had a vision (or contemplation) of the unity of all things in God.

This vision opened up all his faculties to

the creative power of God so that he became the flute through which the Spirit of God breathed, producing music, harmony and praise. He did not think of himself as a monk, but as a brother ('friar') to all, showing that all God's people could become instruments of God's love to each other, and prayer could become the resounding music of human life.

Fourth, Francis was a man of compassion. Zealous people are often bigoted and lacking in charity, but Francis combined zeal with compassion. This lovely word means that he possessed a fellow-feeling for all God's creatures – a passion which shared tears and laughter with the profound sorrows and ecstasies of being alive. This compassion was infectious, for many men and women gathered around him and caught his flame and glory.

Birds and animals listened to his voice, wild creatures fell under his spell, and warring factions were brought to reconciliation and peace. In the awful days of crusades he went out to Egypt unarmed, and in the camps of warring Christians and Muslims he preached the Prince of Peace.

This is not the measure of the man – he was far more than this – but it is clear that he is the kind of man, under Christ, that our world needs today.

He continues to be an instrument of God's peace, and some of the loveliest moments of his life are pictured in the following extracts. The story can be magnified a thousand times, but these stories will give the flavour of his captivating beauty, and will, perhaps, cause the reader to go searching for this Francis who sought the love of God – and found it, rejoicing!

BROTHER RAMON SSF

The Society of St Francis

THE CALL OF CHRIST

A PICTURE OF ST FRANCIS

He was a most eloquent man, a man of cheerful countenance, of kindly aspect; he was immune to cowardice, free of insolence. His speech was peaceable, fiery and sharp; his voice was strong, sweet, clear, and sonorous. His skin was delicate, his flesh very spare. He wore rough garments, he slept but very briefly, he gave most generously. And because he was very humble, he showed all mildness to all, adapting himself usefully to the behaviour of all. The more holy amongst the holy, among sinners he was as one of them.

Celano, First Life, 83

THE BEGINNING OF FRANCIS' CONVERSION

Even as a young man Francis had an open-handed sympathy for the poor. One time he was caught in a rush of business, and contrary to his custom, he sent away a beggar who had begged an alms for the love of God without giving him anything. Then he realized what he had done and he ran after him immediately and gave him a generous alms. There and then he promised God that he would never again refuse anyone who asked for love of him, as long as he had anything to give... Afterwards when he had put on the person of Christ Jesus to perfection, he used to say that even when he was in the world, he could scarcely ever hear anyone mention the love of God without being deeply affected.

Bonaventure, Major Life,

'GO AND REPAIR MY HOUSE'

Francis left the town to meditate out-of-doors and as he was passing by the church of San Damiano which was threatening to collapse with age, he felt urged to go in and pray. There, as he knelt in prayer before a painted image of the Crucified, he felt greatly comforted in spirit and his eyes were full of tears as he gazed at the cross. Then, all of a sudden, he heard a voice coming from the cross and telling him three times, 'Francis, go and repair my house. You see it is all falling down.' Francis was terrified at the sound of the voice, but the power of its message penetrated his heart and he went into an ecstasy. Eventually he came back to himself and prepared to obey the command he had received. He was quite willing to devote himself to repairing the ruined church of San Damiano, although the message really referred to the universal Church which Christ 'won for himself at the price of his own blood', as the Holy Spirit afterwards made him realize.

Bonaventure, Major Life

A LIFE TRANSFORMED

This is how God inspired me, Brother Francis, to
embark upon a life of penance. When I was in
sin, the sight of lepers nauseated me beyond
measure; but then God Himself led me into their
company, and I had pity on them. When I had
once become acquainted with them, what had
previously nauseated me became a source of
spiritual and physical consolation for me. After
that I did not wait long before leaving the world.

The Testament of St Francis

POSSESSIONS AND WEAPONS

The Bishop received Francis with kindness, but said: 'It seems to me that it is very hard and difficult to possess nothing in the world.' To this blessed Francis replied, 'My Lord, if we had any possessions we should also be forced to have arms to protect them, since possessions are a cause of disputes and strife, and in many ways we should be hindered from loving God and our neighbour. Therefore in this life we wish to have no temporal possessions.'

Legend of the Three Companions, 33

WISDOM AND VIRTUE

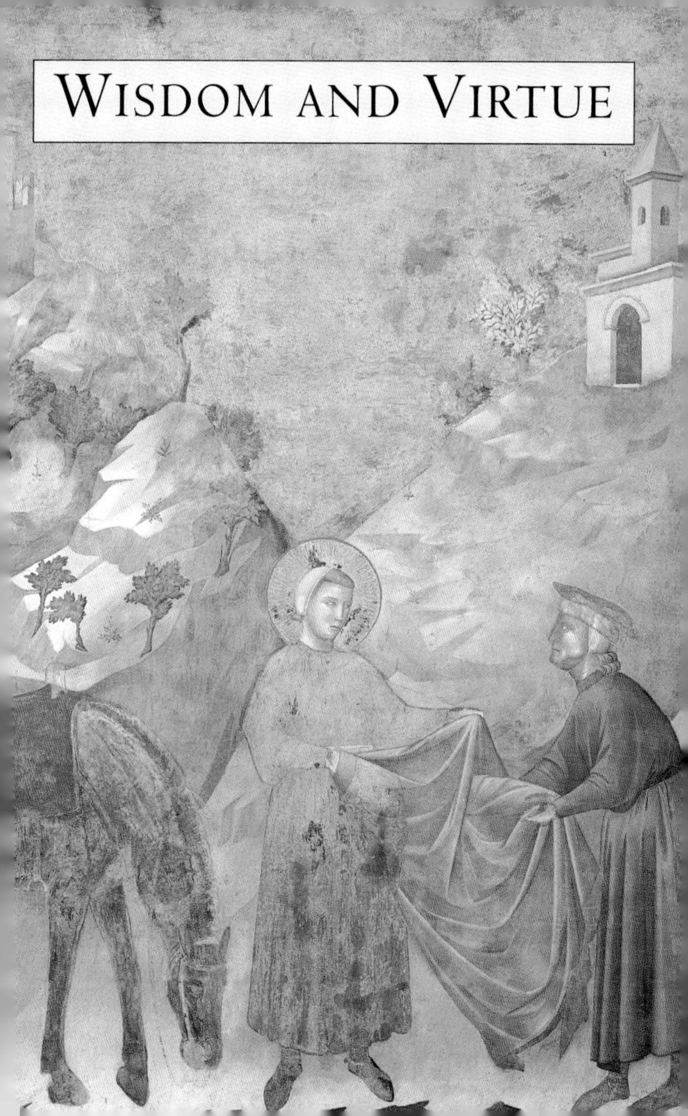

THE PRAISES OF THE VIRTUES

Hail, Queen Wisdom! The Lord save you,
   with your sister, pure, holy Simplicity.
Lady Holy Poverty, God keep you,
   with your sister, holy Humility.
Lady Holy Love, God keep you,
   with your sister, holy Obedience.
All holy virtues,
   God keep you,
   God, from whom you proceed and come.
In all the world there is not a man
   who can possess any one of you
   without first dying to himself.
The man who practises one and does not
   offend against the others possesses all;
The man who offends against one,
   possesses none and violates all.
Each and every one of you
   puts vice and sin to shame.
Holy Wisdom puts Satan
   and all his wiles to shame.

Pure and holy Simplicity puts
    all the learning of this world,
    all natural wisdom, to shame.
Holy Poverty puts to shame
    all greed, avarice,
    and all the anxieties of this life.
Holy Humility puts pride to shame,
    and all the inhabitants of this world
    and all that is in the world.
Holy Love puts to shame all the temptations
    of the devil and the flesh
    and all natural fear.
Holy Obedience puts to shame
    all natural and selfish desires.
It mortifies our lower nature
    and makes it obey the Spirit
    and our fellow men.
Obedience subjects a man
    to everyone on earth,
And not only to men,
    but to all the beasts as well
    and to the wild animals,
So that they can do what they like with him,
    as far as God allows them.

Writings of St Francis

VIRTUE AND VICE

Where there is Love and Wisdom,
    there is neither Fear nor Ignorance.
Where there is Patience and Humility,
    there is neither Anger nor Annoyance.
Where there is Poverty and Joy,
    there is neither Cupidity nor Avarice.
Where there is Peace and Contemplation,
    there is neither Care nor Restlessness.
Where there is the Fear of God
    to guard the dwelling,
    there no enemy can enter.
Where there is Mercy and Prudence,
    there is neither Excess nor Harshness.

Writings of St Francis

TRUE LOVE

Blessed that friar who
loves his brother as much
when he is sick and can
be of no use to him as
when he is well and can be
of use to him. Blessed that
friar who loves and respects
his brother as much when
he is absent as when he is
present and who would not
say anything behind his
back that he could not say
charitably to his face.

Writings of St Francis

TRUE FORGIVENESS

There should be no friar in the whole world who has fallen into sin, no matter how far he has fallen, who will ever fail to find your forgiveness for the asking, if he will only look into your eyes. And if he does not ask forgiveness, you should ask him if he wants it. And should he appear before you again a thousand times, you should love him more than you love me, so that you may draw him to God; you should always have pity on such friars.

St Francis' Letter to a Minister

TRUE PATIENCE

We can never tell how patient or humble a person is when everything is going well with him. But when those who should co-operate with him do the exact opposite, then we can tell. A man has as much patience and humility as he has then, and no more.

Writings of St Francis

LOVE YOUR ENEMIES

Our Lord says in the Gospel, *Love your enemies* (Matthew 5:44). A man really loves his enemy when he is not offended by the injury done to himself, but for love of God feels burning sorrow for the sin his enemy has brought on his own soul, and proves his love in a practical way.

Writings of St Francis

GOD IN ALL CREATION

THE CANTICLE OF BROTHER SUN

Most high, all-powerful, all-good Lord!
    All praise is yours, all glory, all honour
    And all blessing.
To you, alone, Most High, do they belong.
    No mortal lips are worthy
    To pronounce your name.
All praise be yours, my Lord, through all that
    you have made,
    And first my lord Brother Sun,
    Who brings the day; and light you give to
    us through him.
    Of you, Most High, he bears the likeness.
All praise be yours, my Lord, through Sisters
    Moon and Stars;
    In the heavens you have made them, bright
    And precious and fair.
All praise be yours, my Lord, through Brothers
    Wind and Air,
    And fair and stormy, all the weather's moods,
    By which you cherish all that you have made.

All praise be yours, my Lord, through Sister Water,
   So useful, lowly, precious and pure.
All praise be yours, my Lord, through Brother Fire,
   Through whom you brighten up the night...
All praise be yours, my Lord, through Sister
      Earth, our mother,
   Who feeds us in her sovereignty and produces
   Various fruits with coloured flowers and herbs.
All praise be yours, my Lord, through those who
      grant pardon,
   For love of you; through those who endure
   Sickness and trial.
Happy those who endure in peace,
   By you, Most High, they will be crowned.
All praise be yours, my Lord,
      through Sister Death,
   From whose embrace no mortal can escape.
Woe to those who die in mortal sin!
   Happy those she finds doing your will!
   The second death can do no harm to them.
Praise and bless my Lord, and give him thanks,
   And serve him with great humility.

Writings of St Francis

FRANCIS' LADDER OF PRAYER

No human tongue could describe the passionate love with which Francis burned for Christ... He sought to love God in everything. He delighted in all the works of God's hands and from the vision of joy on earth his mind soared aloft to the life-giving source and cause of all. In everything beautiful, he saw him who is beauty itself, and he followed his Beloved everywhere by his likeness imprinted on creation; of all creation he made a ladder by which he might mount up and embrace Him who is all-desirable. He seemed to perceive a divine harmony in the interplay of powers and faculties given by God to his creatures.

Bonaventure, Major Life

BROTHER FIRE, BURN GENTLY

On one occasion the doctors were anxious to perform a cauterization and the friars insisted that Francis should have it done... They sent for a surgeon and he put a searing-iron in the fire in preparation for the operation. Francis trembled with fear, but then he began to encourage his body, addressing the fire like a friend, 'My brother fire, your splendour is the envy of all creation. The Most High made you strong, beautiful and useful. Be gentle to me now, be kind. I beg the great God who created you to temper your heat, so that you will burn gently and I may endure it.' When he had finished his prayer, he made the sign of the cross over the red hot instrument and waited unafraid.

Bonaventure, Major Life

FRANCIS PREACHES TO THE BIRDS

When he was near Bevagna, he came to a huge
flock of birds of various kinds. He ran to them
and greeted them, and they all turned towards him
and waited for him. Those that had perched on
the bushes bent their heads and looked at him in
an extraordinary way. He appealed to them to hear
the word of God saying, 'My brothers, you have a
great obligation to praise your Creator. He clothed
you with feathers and gave you wings to fly,
appointing the clear air as your home, and he
looks after you without any effort on your part.'
The birds showed their pleasure in a wonderful
fashion; they stretched out their necks and flapped
their wings, gazing at him with their beaks open.
In his spiritual enthusiasm Francis walked among
them, brushing them with his habit, and not one
of them moved until he made the sign of the cross
and gave them permission to go. Then they all
flew away together with his blessing.

Bonaventure, Major Life

SHEEP AMONG GOATS

Once, in the Marches of Ancona, Francis found a certain shepherd feeding a herd of she-goats and he-goats in the fields. Among the great number of these goats there was one little lamb going along and feeding humbly and quietly. When blessed Francis saw it, he stopped and, touched inwardly with sorrow of heart and groaning deeply, he said to the brother who was with him, 'Do you not see this sheep that walks so meekly among the goats? I tell you that our Lord Jesus Christ walked in the same way meekly and humbly among the pharisees and chief priests. Therefore I ask you, my son, for the love of him, to have pity with me on this little sheep. Let us pay the price and lead her away from among these goats.'

Celano, First Life, 77

THE GOODNESS OF GOD

Almighty, most high and supreme God, Father, holy and just, Lord, King of heaven and earth, we give you thanks for yourself. Of your own holy will you created all things spiritual and physical, made us in your own image and likeness, and gave us a place in paradise, through your only Son, in the Holy Spirit.

Writings of St Francis

INNER HOLINESS

Go Your Way, Brother Fly

In the early days of the Order, when the brothers lived at Rivo Torto, there was a brother who prayed little and did no work, who never went begging, for he was ashamed, but he ate well. Considering his behaviour, blessed Francis was warned by the Holy Spirit that this brother was a sensual man. One day he said to him: 'Go your way, Brother Fly, for you wish to eat the fruit of the labour of your brothers, while you remain idle in the vineyard of God. You resemble Brother Drone who gathers nothing, does no work, but eats the fruit of the activity of the working bees.' He left without even asking forgiveness, for he was a sensual man.

Legend of Perugia, 62

FRANCIS REBUKES A GLOOMY FRIAR

Why are you making an outward display of grief and sorrow for your sin? This sorrow is between God and yourself alone. So pray Him in His mercy to pardon you and restore to your soul the joy of His salvation, of which the guilt of your sins has deprived it. Always do your best to be cheerful when you are with me and the other brethren; it is not right for a servant of God to show a sad and gloomy face to his brother or to anyone else.

Mirror of Perfection, 96

INWARD INTEGRITY

During winter, when Francis' small, holy body was covered only with a single tunic, patched quite fully with poor pieces of cloth, his guardian obtained a skin of a fox and giving it to him, said: 'Father, you are suffering from an infirmity of the spleen and stomach; I pray you, in your love for the Lord, let this skin be sewn beneath your tunic. If the whole skin does not please you, then at least let a part of it be put over your stomach.' St Francis replied to him, 'If you want me to permit this under my tunic, then have a piece of the same size attached to the outside, which, sewn on the outside, will show men that there is a skin hidden inside too.'

Celano, Second Life, 130

THE WISDOM OF THE HEART

We must all be on our guard against pride and empty boasting and beware of worldly or natural wisdom. A worldly spirit loves to talk a lot but do nothing, striving for the exterior signs of holiness that people can see, with no desire for true piety and interior holiness of spirit. It was about people like this that our Lord said, *Amen I say to you, they have received their reward* (Matthew 6:2). The spirit of God, on the other hand, inspires us to... humility, patience, perfect simplicity, and true peace of heart.

Writings of St Francis

THE FIRE OF WITNESS

A famous theologian asked Francis to interpret the text of Ezekiel: *'If thou proclaim not to the wicked man his wickedness, I will require his soul at thy hand.'*

Francis said: 'I would take it that the servant of God should be so aflame in his life and his holiness that he would reprove all wicked men by the light of his example and by the words of his conversation. So I say, the splendour of his life and the renown of his fame will proclaim to all their wickedness.' That man, therefore, went away much edified, and he said to the companions of Francis: 'My brothers, the theology of this man, based upon purity of life and contemplation, is a soaring eagle; but our learning crawls on its belly on the ground.'

Celano, Second Life, 103

OUR BODY IS OUR CELL

Wherever we are, wherever we go, we bring our cell with us. Our brother body is our cell and our soul is the hermit living in that cell in order to pray to God and meditate. If our soul does not live in peace and solitude within its cell, of what avail is it to live in a man-made cell?

Legend of Perugia, 80

WHOLE-HEARTED DEVOTION

Most holy, our Creator and Redeemer, our Saviour and our Comforter...

May we love you with our whole heart by always thinking of you; with our whole mind by directing our whole intention towards you and seeking your glory in everything; and with all our strength by spending all our energies and affections of soul and body in the service of your love alone.

Writings of St Francis

THE MELODY
OF THE SPIRIT

JOY AND TEARS

When the sweetest melody of spirit would
bubble up in him, Francis would give exterior
expression to it in a song of joy. At times, as
we saw with our own eyes, he would pick up a
stick from the ground and putting it over his
left arm, would draw across it as across a
violin, a little bow bent by means of a string;
and going through the motions of playing, he
would sing in French about his Lord. This
whole ecstasy of joy would often end in tears
and his song of gladness would be dissolved in
compassion for the passion of Christ. Then
this saint would bring forth continual sighs,
and amid deep groanings, he would be raised
up to heaven, forgetful of the lower things he
held in his hand.

Celano, Second Life, 127

THE CRIB AT GRECCIO

There was a certain man by the name of John. Francis sent for this man, and said: 'If you want us to celebrate the feast of our Lord at Greccio, go with haste and diligently prepare what I tell you. For I wish to do something that will recall to memory the little Child who was born in Bethlehem…' When the good and faithful man heard these things, he ran with haste and prepared in that place all the things the saint had told him.

The manger was prepared, the hay had been brought, the ox and ass were led in. There simplicity was honoured, poverty was exalted, humility was commended, and Greccio was made, as it were, a new Bethlehem. The people came and were filled with new joy over the mystery. The woods rang with the voices of the crowd and the rocks made answer to their jubilation. The brothers sang, and the whole night resounded with their rejoicing. The saint of God stood before the manger, uttering sighs, overcome with love, and filled with a wonderful happiness.

Celano, First Life, 85

PRAISES OF GOD

You are holy, Lord, the only God,
   and your deeds are wonderful.
You are strong.
   You are great.
   You are the Most High,
   You are almighty.
   You, holy Father, are
   King of heaven and earth.
You are Three and One,
   Lord God, all good.
   You are Good, all Good, supreme Good,
   Lord God, living and true.
You are love,
   You are wisdom.
   You are humility,
   You are endurance.
   You are rest,
   You are peace.
   You are joy and gladness,
   You are justice and moderation.
   You are all our riches,
   And you suffice for us.

You are beauty.
　　You are gentleness.
　　You are our protector,
　　You are our guardian and defender.
　　You are courage.
　　You are our haven and our hope.
You are our faith,
　　Our great consolation.
　　You are our eternal life,
　　Great and wonderful Lord,
　　God almighty,
　　Merciful Saviour.

Writings of St Francis

FRANCIS AND CLARE ON FIRE WITH LOVE

While they were sitting there, in a rapture, with their eyes and hands raised to Heaven, it seemed to the men of Assisi and Bettona that the Church of St Mary of the Angels and the forest around the place were all aflame… Consequently the men of Assisi ran down there in great haste to save the Place and put out the fire…

But when they reached the place, they found St Francis with St Clare and all the companions sitting around that very humble table, rapt in God by contemplation and invested with power from on high. Then they knew for sure that it had been a heavenly fire that God had miraculously shown them to symbolize the fire of divine love which was burning in the souls of those holy friars and nuns.

Little Flowers of St Francis, 15

THE WOUNDS OF JESUS

Suddenly, from the height of heaven, a Seraph having six wings of flame swept down towards Francis. It appeared in the image of a man hanging on a cross. Two wings at the head, two others served for flight, and the last two covered the body. It was Christ Himself, who, in order to manifest Himself to the blessed one, appeared in this guise. It fixed Francis with its gaze, then left him, having imprinted on his flesh the living Stigmata of the Crucifixion. From this moment, indeed, Francis was marked with the wounds of the Divine Redeemer. His feet, his hands seemed pierced with nails of which the round black heads appeared in the palms of the hands, and on the feet, the points thrust through the flesh bent back. And there, too, on the right side, was a wound as though made by a lance, from which the blood frequently oozed, even through his shirt and tunic.

Bonaventure, Major Life

SEARCHING FOR FRANCIS

Nikos Kazantsakis pictures Francis sitting in the wintry sun at the Portiuncula Church of St Mary and the Angels. A young man comes running up to him, breathless, and stands before him:

'Where is Francis, Bernadone's son?' he asked, his tongue hanging out of his mouth. 'Where can I find the new saint so that I may fall at his feet? For months now I have been roaming the streets looking for him. For the love of Christ, my brother, tell me where he is.'

'Where is Francis, Bernadone's son?' replied Francis, shaking his head. 'Where is Francis, Bernadone's son? What is this Francis? Who is he? I am looking for him also, my brother. I have been looking for him now for years. Give me your hand; let us go find him.'

Brother Ramon SSF, Franciscan Spirituality, sf